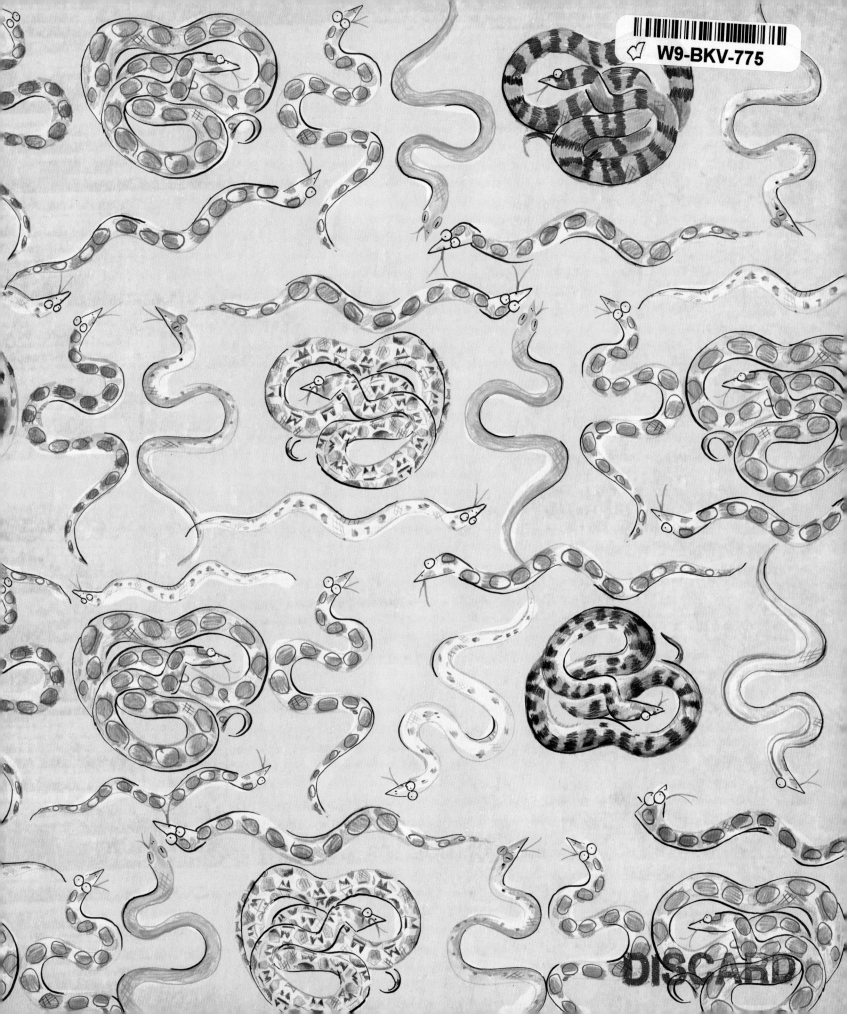

For Toes and Gee, Poborsky and Solskjaer — the geckos, the corn snake around the lightbulb, and the rat snake under the floorboards
N. D.

For my nephew, Raul
L. L.

Text copyright © 2015 by Nicola Davies
Illustrations copyright © 2015 by Luciano Lozano

First U.S. edition 2015

Library of Congress Catalog Card Number 2014951799
ISBN 978-0-7636-7831-9

TWP 20 19 18 17 16 15
10 9 8 7 6 5 4 3 2 1

Printed in Johor Bahru, Malaysia

This book was typeset in Ashley Script and VAG Rounded.
The illustrations were done in mixed media.

Candlewick Press
99 Dover Street
Somerville, Massachusetts 02144

visit us at www.candlewick.com

CANDLEWICK PRESS

Please note: On page 15, the image labeled as a coral snake actually depicts a harmless milk snake, which has a similar pattern of stripes. The error will be corrected in future printings.

I ~~DON'T~~ LIKE SNAKES

Nicola Davies

illustrated by
Luciano Lozano

Some families have dogs, or cats, or birds.
But my family has **SNAKES**. They love them!

So when I said, "I really, *really*,
REALLY don't like snakes!"

they all said,

"WHY?"

"Because," I said, "they slither!"

"Snakes HAVE to slither," said my mom. "They don't have legs, so they bend like an S and use their ribs and scales to grip. It's the only way they can move."

8

Snakes slither in different ways. . . .

Concertina slithering

The snake grips the ground at its tail end with the scales on its underside and stretches forward with its head end.
Then it grips at the head and pulls the tail end forward, and starts all over again.

Serpentine slithering

The snake uses its scales for grip and presses against the ground and against objects
on either side with the curves of its body, to push itself forward.

Caterpillar crawling

When a snake needs to move without any side-to-side wiggling, the scales under its head and neck grip the ground
while its tail end scrunches upward and forward, like an inchworm.

"And look what snakes can do," said Dad. "They can side-wind over sand, twine through trees, swim, climb — even fly!"

"OK," I said. "That's pretty smart."

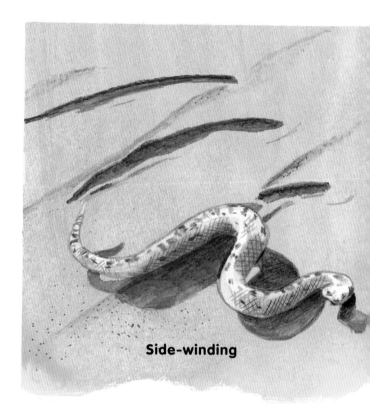

Side-winding

On soft slipping sand, a snake moves by lifting its head and neck off the ground, gripping with just two points on its body and bending like an S between them.

Flying

A few forest-dwelling snakes can flatten their bodies and glide like a floating ribbon from one tree to the next.

Twining

Snakes can twine around branches or
stretch their bodies across big gaps
to move through trees.

Climbing

Gripping with their belly scales and using caterpillar
crawling, snakes can climb tree trunks and walls.

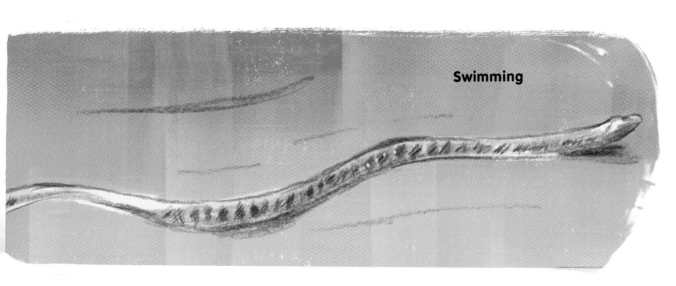

Swimming

Many kinds of
snakes can
swim, and some
live in rivers
and even in
the ocean.

"But what about their slimy, scaly skin? It's icky!"

"Snakes aren't slimy," said Mom. "If you touch a snake's skin, it's dry. It looks wet because snakes have a shiny, see-through outer skin.

When that's worn-out or outgrown, like your old clothes that get too scruffy or too small, the snake just sheds it. And there's new skin underneath."

12

The snake wriggles out of its skin the way you pull your foot out of a sock, leaving the old skin inside out!

snakes even shed the skin covering their eyes

rattlesnakes keep bits of old skin on their tails to make a warning rattle sound when they wiggle

"And as for snakes being scaly," said Dad, "their scales are like armor. They also make mosaic patterns—so a snake can stand out like a warning . . . or almost disappear!"

corn snake

Gaboon viper

coral snake

"OK," I said, "that's pretty cool."

14

A coral snake's stripes are a warning to any animal that might eat it that this snake can bite back!

The color and pattern of the Gaboon viper's scales help it blend in to its surroundings. This is called camouflage, and it allows snakes to hide from animals they want to eat—and from ones that might eat them!

"But I still don't like their flicky tongues!"

"Snakes smell with their tongues," said Mom. "They flick them out to collect smells. All snakes are hunters, and smelling is how they find their prey."

"OK," I said. "That IS interesting."

16

Snakes have two slits in the roof of their mouths, lined with sensitive smell-sensing skin: the Jacobson's organ. This helps snakes detect faint scent trails left by prey and other snakes.

A snake's forked tongue carries the scent trails into the twin slits of the Jacobson's organ. Snakes also pick up airborne scents with their nostrils.

nostril

Jacobson's organ

tongue

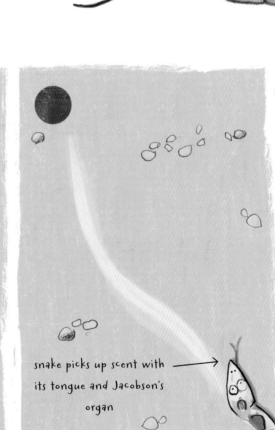

prey's scent trail

snake picks up scent with its tongue and Jacobson's organ

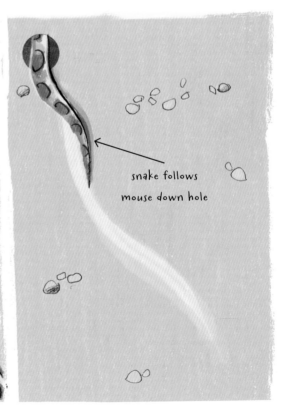

snake follows mouse down hole

17

"But I STILL don't like the way they stare! It's creepy."

"They stare," said Dad, "because they can't blink. Snakes don't have eyelids! But looking at their eyes can tell you how they do their hunting. . . ."

18

Nighttime hunters tend to have slit-shaped pupils. Horizontal slits help snakes that chase prey, like the vine snake, while vertical slits are better for ambush hunters, like the Children's python.

Children's python

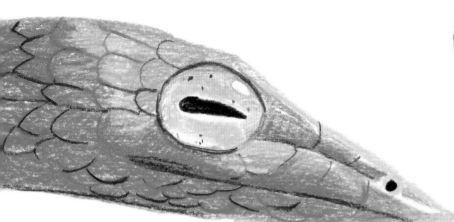

vine snake

Daytime hunters that chase prey, like the fast-moving boomslang, have rounded pupils. The pupils of other daytime hunters, like the slug-eating snake, can shrink to a pinprick to protect sensitive eyes from bright daylight.

slug-eating snake

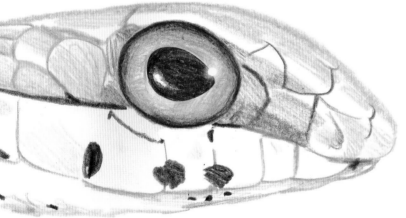

boomslang

Some snakes, like the pit viper, hunt when it's too dark for even the best eyes to see. They have heat-sensitive pits below their eyes so they can feel their prey's body heat.

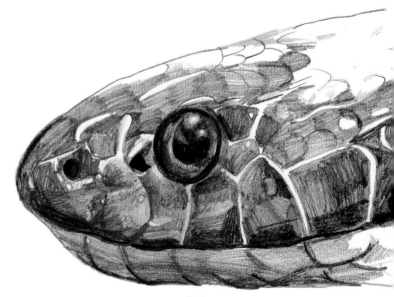

pit viper

"OK," I said. "Maybe now that I know something about them, I do like snakes—just a little bit!"

"You do?" said my brother. "Well, in that case, I'll tell you something that'll really scare you—how they kill things.

Some snakes use **POISON**. They have fangs that are hollow, like a doctor's needle, which inject venom. They strike like lightning, killing with just one bite. Their dinner dies in moments.

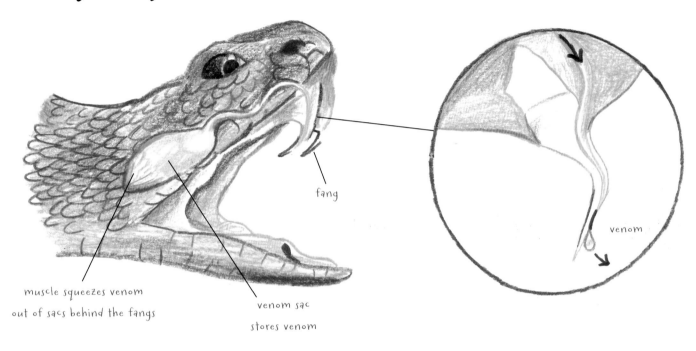

fang

muscle squeezes venom
out of sacs behind the fangs

venom sac
stores venom

venom

Some snakes have a bite so venomous it can kill a human in minutes.
Only people trained as snake handlers should go near any venomous snake.

Fangs can inject venom with
the smallest pinprick.

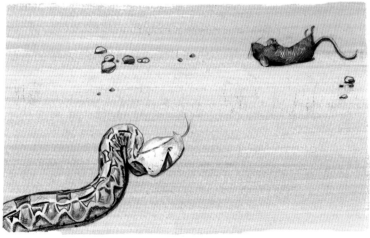

Venom kills fast, so even if the prey runs away it doesn't
get far, and the snake can track it by smell.

Other snakes are **STRANGLERS**—they use their bodies like rope to tie prey up and squeeze the life out of it.

Snakes that kill like this are called constrictors. They wrap their bodies around their prey and squeeze tight until they feel the prey's heart stop beating. Most snakes are shorter than a jump rope and eat mice and rats, but some are big enough to kill animals as large as a deer or kangaroo.

But however snakes kill their prey, there's only one way they can eat it. They don't have claws to rip food to pieces or the right kind of teeth for chewing, so they have to swallow meals whole! So," my brother said, "what do you think of that?"

"I think that's great!" I said. "What's more, I have something to tell YOU.

It's something I found out MYSELF . . . and that's how snakes have their babies.

Some snakes give birth to live babies. But most lay eggs with leathery shells that can take months to hatch.

Live snakes are born inside a see-through sac that they wriggle out of immediately—and they may stay near their mother for only a few hours.

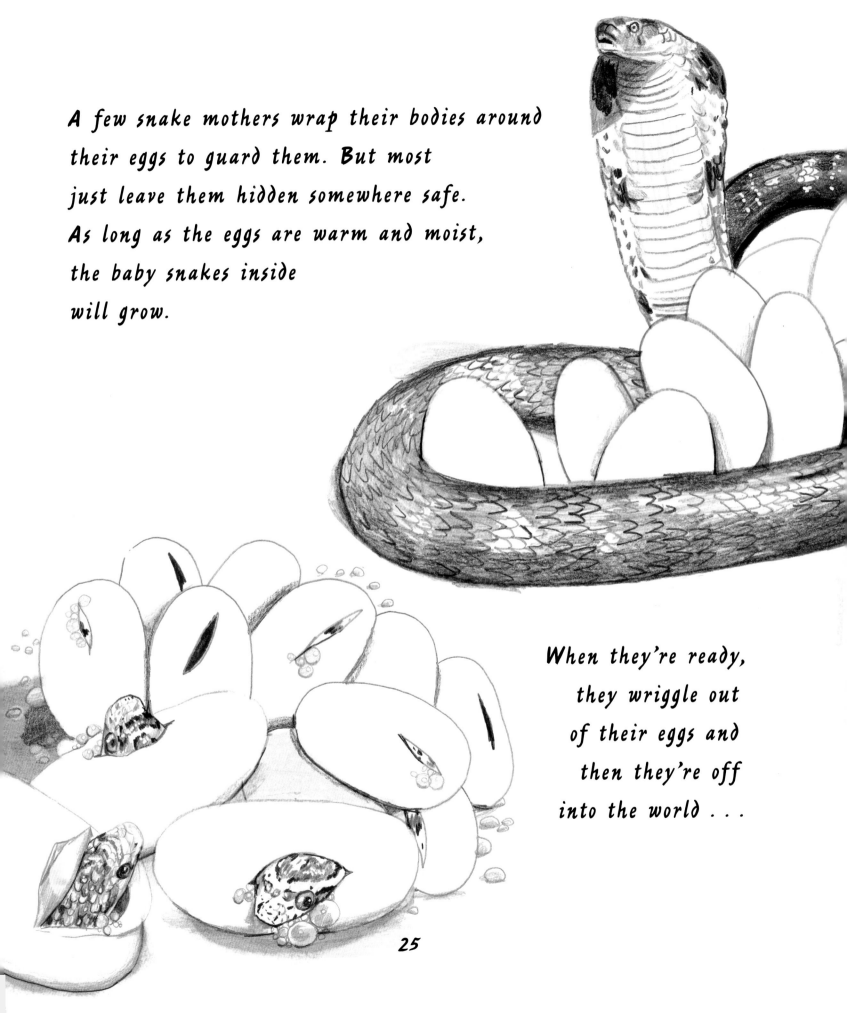

A few snake mothers wrap their bodies around their eggs to guard them. But most just leave them hidden somewhere safe. As long as the eggs are warm and moist, the baby snakes inside will grow.

When they're ready, they wriggle out of their eggs and then they're off into the world . . .

25

slithering . . . tongues flicking . . .
unblinking . . . scaly and shiny
and snaky . . .

and beautiful.

And do you know what?" I said. "I really, really,
REEEEEALLLLY LIKE THEM!"

ALL ABOUT SNAKES

There are almost **3,000** different species (kinds) of snakes in the world. They are found everywhere except for the Arctic and Antarctic, New Zealand, Ireland, and some remote islands in the ocean. Some snakes are as small as a shoelace and some are big enough to swallow a child. They thrive in almost every kind of habitat and can even be found living in the ocean. Their beauty and variety demonstrate the amazing things that can be done with a body that is really just a tube!

BIBLIOGRAPHY

Greene, Harry W. *Snakes: The Evolution of Mystery in Nature.* Berkeley: University of California Press, 1997.

Halliday, Tim, and Kraig Adler, eds. *The New Encyclopedia of Reptiles and Amphibians.* Oxford: Oxford University Press, 2002.

Mattison, Chris. *The New Encyclopedia of Snakes.* Princeton, NJ: Princeton University Press, 2007.

threadsnake
4 in. (10 cm)

green anaconda
22 ft. (6.6 m)

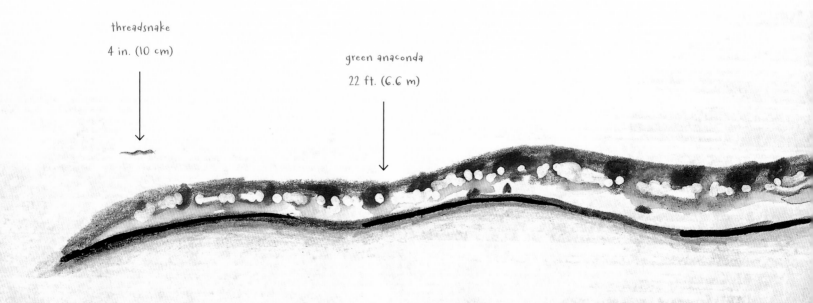

INDEX

Look up the pages to find out about all these snake things.

Don't forget to look at both kinds of words—

this kind and this kind.

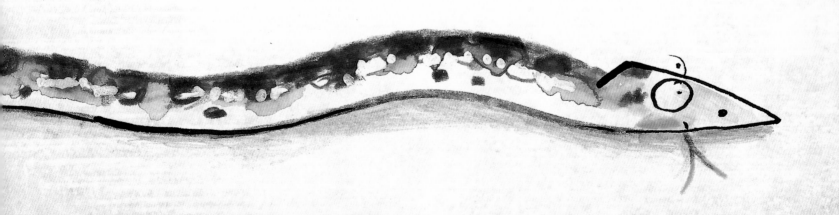

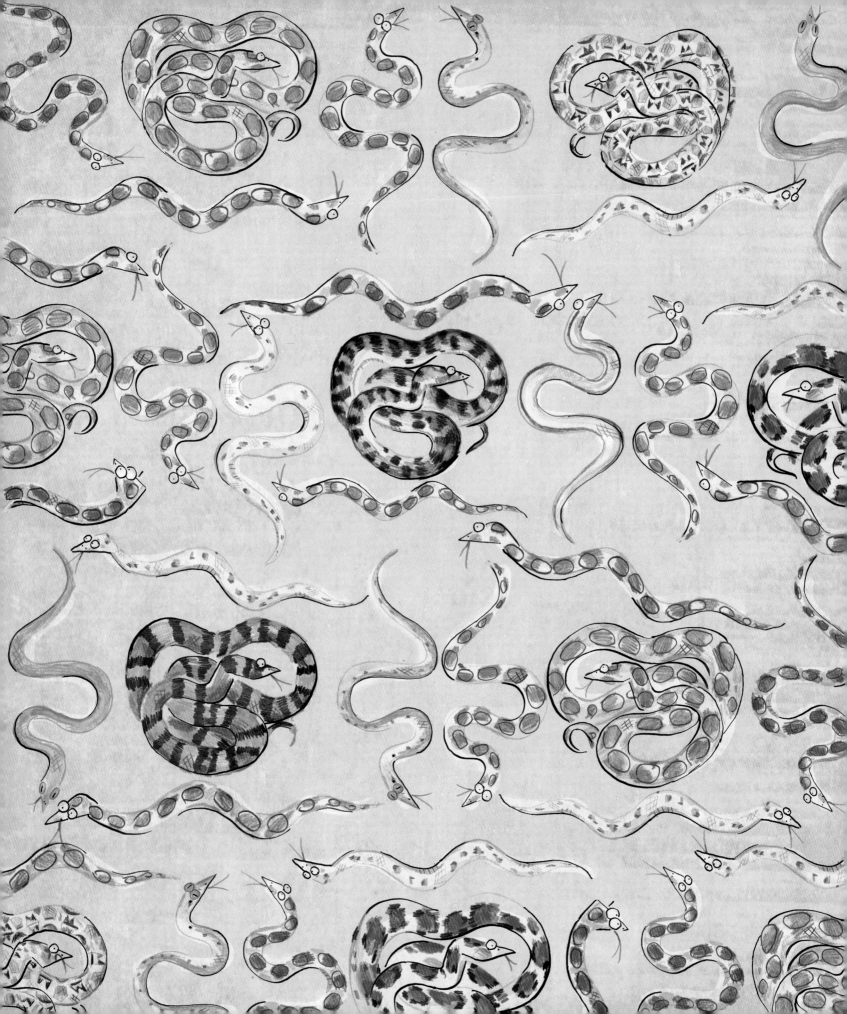